My Readers' Workshop Journal

LEVEL TWO

My Readers' Workshop Journal

NAME:

Section Two

INFERRING CHARACTERS' FEELINGS AND TRAITS

- Noticing The Character's Feelings and Reactions

- Feelings Vs. Traits

- Studying the Character to Infer Traits

- Writing About Reading
  Step 2

♡ Feeling List

HAPPY	PEACEFUL	SAD	ANGRY	SURPRISED	FEARFUL
cheerful	accepted	bored	agitated	amazed	anxious
confident	affectionate	depressed	annoyed	bewildered	embarrassed
content	calm	disappointed	frustrated	confused	excluded
eager	caring	guilty	irritated	curious	frightened
elated	inspired	hopeless	jealous	moved	insecure
energetic	loved	hurt	mad	overwhelmed	nervous
enthusiastic	passionate	inferior	offended	shocked	panicked
excited	relaxed	insignificant		speechless	regretful
hopeful	thankful	lonely		startled	scared
optimistic	thoughtful	miserable		stunned	shy
proud	trusted	rejected			terrified
silly	valued	tired			worried

GENERAL NEGATIVE FEELINGS

afraid	dreadful	stressed out
aggravated	frantic	suspicious
awkward	frozen	tense
concerned	hysterical	threatened
defensive	lost	troubled
desperate	mixed-up	uncomfortable
distressed	self-conscious	unsafe
		vulnerable

GENERAL POSITIVE FEELINGS

accepting	compassionate	overjoyed
ambitious	delightful	pleased
amused	empowered	relieved
appreciated	encouraged	sensitive
brave	grateful	special
capable	interested	strong
careful	joyful	successful
cautious	lucky	understood
cherished	motivated	upbeat
comfortable	okay	vibrant

☐ Group Session   ☐ Class Session   ☐ Independent Reading

Title: _____   Genre: _____
Author: _____   Teacher: _____

 # Trait List

MEAN		NICE		HAPPY		FUNNY
cruel		agreeable		cheerful		amusing
hateful		compassionate		content		comical
impolite		courteous		delighted		hilarious
rude		friendly		excited		humorous
thoughtless		helpful		glad		hysterical
unfriendly		kindhearted		joyful		silly
unkind		pleasant		pleased		
wicked		thoughtful		satisfied		

BRAVE		SMART		TRICKY		DEPRESSED
adventurous		brainy		deceitful		discouraged
courageous		bright		dishonest		gloomy
daring		brilliant		secretive		miserable
fearless		clever		sly		mournful
heroic		intelligent		sneaky		sorrowful
		skillful		untrustworthy		
		wise				

SERIOUS		TALKATIVE		THANKFUL		ACTIVE
competent		chatty		appreciative		athletic
determined		communicative		grateful		energetic
hardworking						
reliable				CLUMSY		SHY
				awkward		bashful
				uncoordinated		quiet

Title: _____   Genre: _____
Author: _____   Teacher: _____

Readers Notice the Character's ♡♡ Feelings and Reactions

Notice The Character		Positive/Negative Feeling	Inferred ♡ Feeling
How s/he acts		👍👎	
How s/he speaks		👍👎	
What s/he says		👍👎	
What s/he thinks		👍👎	

In the book _____ written by _____

the character _____ did/said _____
            (name of character)

_____

_____

I infer the character feels _____

☐ Group Session   ☐ Class Session   ☐ Independent Reading

Readers Notice the Character's ♡♡♡ Feelings and Reactions

Notice The Character		Positive/Negative Feeling	Inferred ♡ Feeling
How s/he acts		👍 👎	
How s/he speaks		👍 👎	
What s/he says		👍 👎	
What s/he thinks		👍 👎	

In the book _____ written by _____

the character _____ did/said _____
　　　　　(name of character)

_____

_____

I infer the character feels _____

Title: _____

Author: _____

Genre: _____

Teacher: _____

Readers Notice the Character's ♡♡♡ Feelings and Reactions

Notice The Character		Positive/Negative Feeling	Inferred ♡ Feeling
How s/he acts		👍 👎	
How s/he speaks		👍 👎	
What s/he says		👍 👎	
What s/he thinks		👍 👎	

In the book _____ written by _____

the character _____ did/said _____

(name of character)

_____

_____

I infer the character feels _____

Title: _____   Genre: _____
Author: _____   Teacher: _____

Feelings vs. Traits
Feelings are fleeting! Traits are steadfast!

Directions: As you discover the main character, keep a log of the character's feelings and traits.

Name of Character: _____	
♡ Feelings	Trait

Title: _____

Author: _____

Feelings vs. Traits
Feelings are fleeting! Traits are steadfast!

Directions: As you discover the main character, keep a log of the character's feelings and traits.

Name of Character: _____	
♡ Feelings	Trait

☐ Group Session   ☐ Class Session   ☐ Independent Reading

Feelings vs. Traits
Feelings are fleeting! Traits are steadfast!

Directions: As you discover the main character, keep a log of the character's feelings and traits.

Name of Character: _____	
♡ Feelings	Trait

Title: _____

Author: _____

Studying the Character to Infer Traits

Feelings

In the text…

_____

_____

_____

_____

Inferred Trait

_____

Action

In the text…

_____

_____

_____

Inferred Trait

CHARACTER

_____

Dialogue

In the text…

_____

_____

_____

_____

_____

_____

Inferred Trait

_____

Thoughts

In the text…

_____

_____

_____

_____

_____

_____

Inferred Trait

_____

☐ Group Session   ☐ Class Session   ☐ Independent Reading

Title: _____   Genre: _____

Author: _____   Teacher: _____

Studying the Character to Infer Traits

Feelings

In the text…

_____

_____

_____

_____

🧠 Inferred Trait

_____

Action

In the text…

_____

_____

_____

🧠 Inferred Trait

CHARACTER

_____

Dialogue

In the text…

_____

_____

_____

_____

🧠 Inferred Trait

_____

Thoughts

In the text…

_____

_____

_____

_____

🧠 Inferred Trait

_____

☐ Group Session   ☐ Class Session   ☐ Independent Reading

Studying the Character to Infer Traits

Feelings

In the text…

_____

_____

_____

_____

🧩 Inferred Trait

_____

Action

In the text…

_____

_____

_____

🧩 Inferred Trait

CHARACTER

_____

Dialogue

In the text…

_____

_____

_____

_____

🧩 Inferred Trait

_____

Thoughts

In the text…

_____

_____

_____

_____

_____

🧩 Inferred Trait

_____

☐ Group Session   ☐ Class Session   ☐ Independent Reading

Title: _____   Genre: _____
Author: _____   Teacher: _____

Readers Study the Character to Infer Traits

The Character Does, Says, or Thinks

Character Trait

_____ → _____
_____

_____ → _____
_____

_____ → _____
_____

_____ → _____
_____

_____ → _____
_____

_____ → _____
_____

_____ → _____
_____

_____ → _____
_____

On your own:

In the book _____ written by _____

the character _____ did/said
                  (name of character)

_____

_____

I infer _____

☐ Group Session   ☐ Class Session   ☐ Independent Reading

Title: _____

Genre: _____

Author: _____

Teacher: _____

Readers Study the Character to Infer Traits

Feeling/trait
_____

Evidence
_____
_____
_____

Feeling/trait
_____

Evidence
_____
_____
_____

Feeling/trait
_____

Evidence
_____
_____
_____

Feeling/trait
_____

Evidence
_____
_____
_____

CHARACTER

_____

Feeling/trait
_____

Evidence
_____
_____
_____

Feeling/trait
_____

Evidence
_____
_____
_____

Feeling/trait
_____

Evidence
_____
_____
_____

Feeling/trait
_____

Evidence
_____
_____
_____

On your own:

In the book _____ written by _____
the character _____ did/said _____
(name of character)
_____
_____
_____

I infer _____

☐ Group Session   ☐ Class Session   ☐ Independent Reading

Title: _____   Genre: _____

Author: _____   Teacher: _____

Character ✦ Traits Reading Response

On your own:

Name of Character: _____

Inferred Trait: _____

Build background of the story (2-3 sentences).

_____

_____

_____

State your inference.

_____

_____

_____

Bring evidence from the story.

_____

_____

_____

✓ Checkbox:

Did I...

☐ Include the title, author, and character's name?

☐ Give a clear background of the story, including only the important parts?

☐ Support my inference with evidence? (Does the evidence match my inference?)

☐ Group Session   ☐ Class Session   ☐ Independent Reading

Title: _____   Genre: _____
Author: _____   Teacher: _____

Character 🧩 Trait Reading Response

📖 <u>On your own:</u>

Character: _____ Inferred Trait: _____

_____

_____

_____

_____

_____

_____

_____

_____

☑ Checkbox:

Did I...

☐ Include the title, author, and character's name?

☐ Give a clear background of the story, including only the important parts?

☐ Support my inference with evidence? (Does the evidence match my inference?)

☐ Group Session   ☐ Class Session   ☐ Independent Reading

Title: _____   Genre: _____
Author: _____   Teacher: _____

Readers Study the Character to Infer Traits

The Character Does, Says, or Thinks

Character Trait

_____ → _____

_____ → _____

_____ → _____

_____ → _____

_____ → _____

_____ → _____

_____ → _____

_____ → _____

On your own:

In the book _____ written by _____

the character _____ did/said
(name of character)

_____

_____

I infer _____

☐ Group Session   ☐ Class Session   ☐ Independent Reading

Title: _____

Author: _____

Genre: _____

Teacher: _____

Readers Study the Character to Infer Traits

Feeling/trait
_____

Evidence
_____
_____
_____

Feeling/trait
_____

Evidence
_____
_____
_____

Feeling/trait
_____

Evidence
_____
_____
_____

Feeling/trait
_____

Evidence
_____
_____

CHARACTER
_____

Feeling/trait
_____

Evidence
_____
_____

Feeling/trait
_____

Evidence
_____
_____
_____

Feeling/trait
_____

Evidence
_____
_____
_____

Feeling/trait
_____

Evidence
_____
_____
_____

On your own:

In the book _____ written by _____

the character _____ did/said _____
(name of character)

_____
_____
_____

I infer _____

Title: _____   Genre: _____
Author: _____   Teacher: _____

Character ⚙ Traits Reading Response

📕 <u>On your own</u>:

Name of Character: _____

Inferred Trait: _____

Build background of the story (2-3 sentences).
_____
_____
_____

State your inference.
_____
_____
_____

Bring evidence from the story.
_____
_____
_____

✅ Checkbox:

Did I...

☐ Include the title, author, and character's name?

☐ Give a clear background of the story, including only the important parts?

☐ Support my inference with evidence? (Does the evidence match my inference?)

☐ Group Session   ☐ Class Session   ☐ Independent Reading

Title: _____   Genre: _____
Author: _____   Teacher: _____

Character 🧩 Trait Reading Response

📖 <u>On your own:</u>

Character: _____ Inferred Trait: _____

_____

_____

_____

_____

_____

_____

_____

_____

☑ Checkbox:

Did I...

☐ Include the title, author, and character's name?

☐ Give a clear background of the story, including only the important parts?

☐ Support my inference with evidence? (Does the evidence match my inference?)

☐ Group Session   ☐ Class Session   ☐ Independent Reading

Title: _____

Genre: _____
Author: _____

Teacher: _____

Readers Study the Character to Infer Traits

The Character Does, Says, or Thinks

Character Trait

_____
_____
_____

→ _____
_____

_____
_____
_____

→ _____
_____

_____
_____
_____

→ _____
_____

_____
_____
_____

→ _____
_____

_____
_____
_____

→ _____
_____

_____
_____
_____

→ _____
_____

_____
_____
_____

→ _____
_____

_____
_____
_____

→ _____
_____

On your own:

In the book _____ written by _____

the character _____ did/said
               (name of character)

_____

_____

I infer _____

Readers Study the Character to Infer 🧩 Traits

Feeling/trait	Feeling/trait	Feeling/trait
_____	_____	_____
Evidence	Evidence 🔍	Evidence
_____	_____	_____
_____	_____	_____
_____	_____	_____

Feeling/trait		Feeling/trait
_____	**CHARACTER**	_____
Evidence		Evidence
_____		_____
_____	_____	_____
_____		_____

Feeling/trait	Feeling/trait	Feeling/trait
_____	_____	_____
Evidence	Evidence	Evidence
_____	_____	_____
_____	_____	_____
_____	_____	_____

On your own:

In the book _____ written by _____
the character _____ did/said _____
_____(name of character)_____

_____

_____

I infer _____

Title: _____   Genre: _____
Author: _____   Teacher: _____

Character ✦ Traits Reading Response

📖 On your own:

Name of Character: _____
Inferred Trait: _____

Build background of the story (2-3 sentences).

_____
_____
_____
_____

State your inference.

_____
_____
_____

Bring evidence from the story.

_____
_____
_____

☑ Checkbox:

Did I...

☐ Include the title, author, and character's name?

☐ Give a clear background of the story, including only the important parts?

☐ Support my inference with evidence? (Does the evidence match my inference?)

☐ Group Session   ☐ Class Session   ☐ Independent Reading

Title: _____   Genre: _____
Author: _____   Teacher: _____

Character 🧩 Trait Reading Response

📖 On your own:

Character: _____ Inferred Trait: _____

_____

_____

_____

_____

_____

_____

_____

_____

☑ Checkbox:

Did I...

☐ Include the title, author, and character's name?

☐ Give a clear background of the story, including only the important parts?

☐ Support my inference with evidence? (Does the evidence match my inference?)

☐ Group Session   ☐ Class Session   ☐ Independent Reading

Following the Character's Journey
Through the Story Mountain

Directions: Follow the character alongside the story mountain.
Write the feeling and trait shown at each point in the story.

Phew!
_____

Oh-Kay
_____

Feeling: _____
Trait: _____

Feeling: _____
Trait: _____

Uh! – Oh!
_____

Uh – Oh
_____

Feeling: _____
Trait: _____

Feeling: _____
Trait: _____

Character/Setting
_____

Feeling: _____
Trait: _____

☐ Group Session   ☐ Class Session   ☐ Independent Reading

Title: _____   Genre: _____
Author: _____   Teacher: _____

Following the Character's Journey
Through the Story Mountain

Directions: Summarize the story using the words first, then, next, after that, finally.
Include the character's trait or feeling at any two points.

_____

_____

_____

_____

_____

_____

_____

_____

_____

_____

_____

_____

☐ Group Session   ☐ Class Session   ☐ Independent Reading

Title: _____   Genre: _____
Author: _____   Teacher: _____

Following the Character's Journey
Through the Story Mountain

Directions: Follow the character alongside the story mountain.
Write the feeling and trait shown at each point in the story.

Oh-Kay

Phew!

Feeling: _____
Trait: _____

Feeling: _____
Trait: _____

Uh! - Oh!

Uh - Oh

Feeling: _____
Trait: _____

Feeling: _____
Trait: _____

Feeling: _____
Trait: _____

Character/Setting

Following the Character's Journey
Through the Story Mountain

Directions: Summarize the story using the words first, then, next, after that, finally.
Include the character's trait or feeling at any two points.

_____

_____

_____

_____

_____

_____

_____

_____

_____

_____

_____

☐ Group Session   ☐ Class Session   ☐ Independent Reading

Title: _____   Genre: _____
Author: _____   Teacher: _____

Following the Character's Journey
Through the Story Mountain

Directions: Follow the character alongside the story mountain.
Write the feeling and trait shown at each point in the story.

Phew!

Oh-Kay

Feeling: _____
Trait: _____

Uh - Oh!

Feeling: _____
Trait: _____

Feeling: _____
Trait: _____

Uh - Oh

Feeling: _____
Trait: _____

Feeling: _____
Trait: _____

Character/Setting

Title: _____   Genre: _____
Author: _____   Teacher: _____

Following the Character's Journey
Through the Story Mountain

Directions: Summarize the story using the words first, then, next, after that, finally.
Include the character's trait or feeling at any two points.

_____

_____

_____

_____

_____

_____

_____

_____

_____

_____

_____

☐ Group Session   ☐ Class Session   ☐ Independent Reading

Section Three

UNDERSTANDING THE CHARACTER THROUGH MAKING CONNECTIONS

- Empathizing to Understand the Character's Motives

- Connecting to the Character's Experiences

- Comparing Reactions, Feelings, and Traits

- Writing about Reading
  Step 3

Readers Empathize to
Understand the Character's Motives

Character: _____

Character's experience	Character's reaction
_____	_____
_____	_____
_____	_____
_____	_____

Yourself in the character's shoes

Your reaction	The trait you showed
_____	_____
_____	_____
_____	_____
_____	_____

Your reaction compared to the character's reaction.

_____

_____

_____

_____

Conculsion: What does this tell you about the character?

_____

_____

_____

_____

☐ Group Session   ☐ Class Session   ☐ Independent Reading

Readers Empathize to
Understand the Character's Motives

On your own:

Paragraph #1:

(Clear background of the story and character's reaction, including the title, author, and character's name)

> In the book _____
> _____
> _____
> _____

Paragraph #2:

(Yourself in the character's shoes)

> If I would be/When I was _____
> _____
> _____
> _____

Paragraph #3:

(Conclusion: Your theory about the character)

> In conclusion, I think _____
> _____

☐ Group Session   ☐ Class Session   ☐ Independent Reading

Title: _____   Genre: _____
Author: _____   Teacher: _____

Readers Empathize to
Understand the Character's Motives

<u>On your own:</u>

Checkbox:

Be sure to include:

- ☐ The title, author, and character's name.
- ☐ A brief background of the story leading up to the problem
- ☐ The character's reaction to the problem
- ☐ Yourself in the character's shoes
- ☐ Your conclusion about the character

_____

_____

_____

_____

_____

_____

_____

_____

_____

_____

☐ Group Session   ☐ Class Session   ☐ Independent Reading

Readers Empathize to Understand the Character's Motives

Character: _____

Character's experience ✨	Character's reaction ☺ ☹

Yourself in the character's shoes

Your reaction ☺ ☹	The trait you showed

Your reaction compared to the character's reaction. ☺ ☹

_____

Conculsion: What does this tell you about the character?

_____

Title: _____   Genre: _____
Author: _____   Teacher: _____

Readers Empathize to
Understand the Character's Motives

On your own:

Paragraph #1:

(Clear background of the story and character's reaction, including the title, author, and character's name)

In the book _____

_____

_____

_____

Paragraph #2:

(Yourself in the character's shoes)

If I would be/When I was _____

_____

_____

_____

Paragraph #3:

(Conclusion: Your theory about the character)

In conclusion, I think _____

_____

☐ Group Session   ☐ Class Session   ☐ Independent Reading

Title: _____

Author: _____

Readers Empathize to
Understand the Character's Motives

<u>On your own:</u>

✓ Checkbox:

Be sure to include:

☐ The title, author, and character's name.

☐ A brief background of the story leading up to the problem

☐ The character's reaction to the problem

☐ Yourself in the character's shoes

☐ Your conclusion about the character

_____

_____

_____

_____

_____

_____

_____

_____

_____

_____

_____

☐ Group Session   ☐ Class Session   ☐ Independent Reading

Title: _____

Author: _____

Genre: _____

Teacher: _____

Readers Empathize to
Understand the Character's Motives

Character: _____

Character's experience ✨	Character's reaction 😊😞
_____	_____
_____	_____
_____	_____

Yourself in the character's shoes

Your reaction 😊😞	The trait you showed
_____	_____
_____	_____
_____	_____

😊😞 Your reaction compared to the character's reaction.

_____
_____
_____

Conculsion: What does this tell you about the character?

_____
_____
_____

☐ Group Session   ☐ Class Session   ☐ Independent Reading

Title: _____ Genre: _____
Author: _____ Teacher: _____

Readers Empathize to
Understand the Character's Motives

On your own:

Paragraph #1:
(Clear background of the story and character's reaction, including the title, author, and character's name)

In the book _____

_____

_____

_____

Paragraph #2:
(Yourself in the character's shoes)

If I would be/When I was _____

_____

_____

_____

Paragraph #3:
(Conclusion: Your theory about the character)

In conclusion, I think _____

_____

☐ Group Session   ☐ Class Session   ☐ Independent Reading

Readers Empathize to
Understand the Character's Motives

On your own:

✓ Checkbox:

Be sure to include:

- ☐ The title, author, and character's name.
- ☐ A brief background of the story leading up to the problem
- ☐ The character's reaction to the problem
- ☐ Yourself in the character's shoes
- ☐ Your conclusion about the character

_____

_____

_____

_____

_____

_____

_____

_____

_____

_____

_____

_____

_____

☐ Group Session   ☐ Class Session   ☐ Independent Reading

Section Four

COMPARING CHARACTERS

- Comparing Characters and their Reactions

- Studying Secondary Characters in Relation to the Main Character

- Learning Lessons Alongside the Character/Moral

- Conflict

- Writing about Reading
  Step 4

Comparing Characters and their Reactions to their Struggles

	Name of Character #1 Title _____	Name of Character #2 Title _____
Physical Trait	_____	_____
Character Trait	_____	_____
Main Problem or Struggle Encountered	_____	_____
Reaction to Problem or Struggle	_____	_____

Characters in Comparison

_____

_____

Characters in Contrast

_____

_____

Title: _____   Genre: _____
Author: _____   Teacher: _____

Comparing Characters and their Interactions

On your own:

Character #1

Paragraph #1: (Title/author/character's name, brief background of the story)

_____
_____
_____
_____

Paragraph #2: (Main problem or struggle and the character's reaction)

_____
_____
_____
_____

Conclusion: (Theory/Trait)

_____
_____

☐ Group Session   ☐ Class Session   ☐ Independent Reading

Title: _____

Author: _____

Comparing Characters and their Interactions

On your own:

Character #2

Paragraph #1: (Title/author/character's name, brief background of the story)

Paragraph #2: (Main problem or struggle and the character's reaction)

Conclusion: (Theory/Trait)

In conclusion _____ in the book _____ and
    (name of character #1)   (book title)

_____ in the book _____ are _____
    (name of character #2)   (book title)   (similar/different)

because _____

_____

☐ Group Session   ☐ Class Session   ☐ Independent Reading

Title: _____ Genre: _____
Author: _____ Teacher: _____

Readers Compare Characters and their Reactions

On your own: Be sure to include:

☐ The title, author, and character's name.

☐ A brief background of the story leading up to the problem or struggle

☐ The character's reaction

☐ Your theory about the character

Title: _____   Genre: _____
Author: _____   Teacher: _____

Comparing Characters and their
Reactions to their Struggles

	Name of Character #1 Title _____	Name of Character #2 Title _____
👀 Physical Trait	_____ _____	_____ _____
🧩 Character Trait	_____ _____	_____ _____
⚠ Main Problem or Struggle Encountered	_____ _____ _____ _____	_____ _____ _____ _____
😮 Reaction to Problem or Struggle	_____ _____ _____ _____	_____ _____ _____ _____

👫 Characters in Comparison

_____

_____

Characters in Contrast

_____

_____

Title: _____   Genre: _____
Author: _____   Teacher: _____

Comparing Characters and their Interactions

On your own:

Character #1

Paragraph #1: (Title/author/character's name, brief background of the story)

_____
_____
_____
_____

Paragraph #2: (Main problem or struggle and the character's reaction)

_____
_____
_____
_____
_____

Conclusion: (Theory/Trait)

_____
_____

☐ Group Session   ☐ Class Session   ☐ Independent Reading

Title: _____   Genre: _____
Author: _____   Teacher: _____

Comparing Characters and their Interactions

On your own: Character #2

Paragraph # 1: (Title/author/character's name, brief background of the story)

_____
_____
_____
_____

Paragraph #2: (Main problem or struggle and the character's reaction)

_____
_____
_____
_____

Conclusion: (Theory/Trait)

_____
_____

In conclusion _____ in the book _____ and _____
          (name of character #1)   (book title)

_____ in the book _____ are _____
(name of character #2)   (book title)   (similar/different)

because _____

_____

☐ Group Session   ☐ Class Session   ☐ Independent Reading

Title: _____

Author: _____

Genre: _____

Teacher: _____

Readers Compare Characters and their Reactions

On your own: Be sure to include:

☐ The title, author, and character's name.

☐ A brief background of the story leading up to the problem or struggle

☐ The character's reaction

☐ Your theory about the character

_____

_____

☐ Group Session   ☐ Class Session   ☐ Independent Reading

Title: _____   Genre: _____
Author: _____   Teacher: _____

Comparing Characters and their Reactions to their Struggles

	Name of Character #1 Title _____	Name of Character #2 Title _____
👀 Physical Trait	_____	_____
🧩 Character Trait	_____	_____
⚠️ Main Problem or Struggle Encountered	_____ _____ _____	_____ _____ _____
😮 Reaction to Problem or Struggle	_____ _____ _____	_____ _____ _____

👫 Characters in Comparison

_____

_____

Characters in Contrast

_____

_____

☐ Group Session   ☐ Class Session   ☐ Independent Reading

Title: _____   Genre: _____
Author: _____   Teacher: _____

Comparing Characters and their Interactions

On your own:

Character #1

Paragraph #1: (Title/author/character's name, brief background of the story)

_____
_____
_____
_____

Paragraph #2: (Main problem or struggle and the character's reaction)

_____
_____
_____
_____

Conclusion: (Theory/Trait)

_____
_____

☐ Group Session   ☐ Class Session   ☐ Independent Reading

Title: _____   Genre: _____
Author: _____   Teacher: _____

Comparing Characters and their Interactions

On your own: Character #2

Paragraph #1: (Title/author/character's name, brief background of the story)

_____
_____
_____
_____

Paragraph #2: (Main problem or struggle and the character's reaction)

_____
_____
_____
_____

Conclusion: (Theory/Trait)

_____
_____

In conclusion _____ in the book _____ and ____
              (name of character #1)   (book title)
_____ in the book _____ are _____
(name of character #2)   (book title)   (similar/different)
because _____
_____

☐ Group Session   ☐ Class Session   ☐ Independent Reading

Readers Compare Characters and their Reactions

On your own: Be sure to include:

☐ The title, author, and character's name.

☐ A brief background of the story leading up to the problem or struggle

☐ The character's reaction

☐ Your theory about the character

Title: _____

Author: _____

Genre: _____

Teacher: _____

Readers Study Secondary Characters in Relation to the Main Character

Main Character	Secondary Character
_____	_____

Directions: Follow the secondary character along the story.

Write his/her character trait shown in each part. Considering how it affects the main character,

circle the smile/frown to represent the relationship between the two characters.

Beginning	Then	After that	Next	At the End
☺ ☹	☺ ☹	☺ ☹	☺ ☹	☺ ☹
_____	_____	_____	_____	_____

The Secondary Character's Actions Caused the Main Character to

Feel	_____
Think/Say	_____
Act	_____

Theory about _____.
(Secondary Character)

_____
_____

Theory about _____
(Main Character)

_____
_____

☐ Group Session   ☐ Class Session   ☐ Independent Reading

Title: _____   Genre: _____
Author: _____   Teacher: _____

Readers Compare Characters and their Reactions

<u>On your own</u>:

Be sure to include:

☐ The title, author, and character's name.

☐ A brief background of the story leading up to the problem or struggle

☐ A trait for secondary character and one example where it's proven

☐ The main character's reaction to the secondary character

_____

_____

_____

_____

_____

_____

_____

_____

_____

_____

_____

☐ Group Session   ☐ Class Session   ☐ Independent Reading

Title: _____

Author: _____

Genre: _____

Teacher: _____

Readers Study Secondary Characters in Relation to the Main Character

Main Character	Secondary Character
_____	_____

<u>Directions:</u> Follow the secondary character along the story.

Write his/her character trait shown in each part. Considering how it affects the main character,

circle the smile/frown to represent the relationship between the two characters.

Beginning	Then	After that	Next	At the End
_____	_____	_____	_____	_____

The Secondary Character's Actions Caused the Main Character to

Feel	_____
Think/Say	_____
Act	_____

Theory about _____.
(Secondary Character)

_____
_____

Theory about _____.
(Main Character)

_____
_____

☐ Group Session   ☐ Class Session   ☐ Independent Reading

Readers Compare Characters and their Reactions

On your own:

Be sure to include:

☐ The title, author, and character's name.

☐ A brief background of the story leading up to the problem or struggle

☐ A trait for secondary character and one example where it's proven

☐ The main character's reaction to the secondary character

_____

_____

_____

_____

_____

_____

_____

_____

_____

_____

_____

☐ Group Session   ☐ Class Session   ☐ Independent Reading

Readers Study Secondary Characters in Relation to the Main Character

Main Character	Secondary Character
_____	_____

<u>Directions:</u> Follow the secondary character along the story.

Write his/her character trait shown in each part. Considering how it affects the main character,

circle the smile/frown to represent the relationship between the two characters.

Beginning	Then	After that	Next	At the End

The Secondary Character's Actions Caused the Main Character to

Feel	_____
Think/Say	_____
Act	_____

Theory about _____.
(Secondary Character)

_____
_____

Theory about _____.
(Main Character)

_____
_____

☐ Group Session ☐ Class Session ☐ Independent Reading

Title: _____   Genre: _____
Author: _____   Teacher: _____

Readers Compare Characters and their Reactions

On your own:

Be sure to include:

- ☐ The title, author, and character's name.
- ☐ A brief background of the story leading up to the problem or struggle
- ☐ A trait for secondary character and one example where it's proven
- ☐ The main character's reaction to the secondary character

_____

_____

_____

_____

_____

_____

_____

_____

_____

_____

_____

☐ Group Session   ☐ Class Session   ☐ Independent Reading

Readers Learn Lessons Alongside the Character

Choose your three most favorite books.
Think of the lesson the character learned and how it made an impact on you.

	Title	Struggle	Lesson
BOOK 1	_____	_____ _____ _____	_____ _____ _____
BOOK 2	_____	_____ _____ _____	_____ _____ _____
BOOK 3	_____	_____ _____ _____	_____ _____ _____

☐ Group Session   ☐ Class Session   ☐ Independent Reading

Readers Learn Lessons Alongside the Character

<u>On your own:</u>

Each paragraph should include:

- ☐ The title, author, and character's name.
- ☐ A brief background of the story leading up to the problem or struggle
- ☐ Choose one character from whom you learned a lesson.
- ☐ Write a struggle the character faced and what it taught you.

_____

_____

_____

_____

_____

_____

_____

_____

_____

_____

_____

Title: _____   Genre: _____
Author: _____   Teacher: _____

Readers Learn Lessons Alongside the Character

Choose your three most favorite books.
Think of the lesson the character learned and how it made an impact on you.

	Title	Struggle	Lesson
BOOK 1	_____	_____ _____	_____ _____
BOOK 2	_____	_____ _____	_____ _____
BOOK 3	_____	_____ _____	_____ _____

☐ Group Session   ☐ Class Session   ☐ Independent Reading

Readers Learn Lessons Alongside the Character

On your own:

Each paragraph should include:

- ☐ The title, author, and character's name.
- ☐ A brief background of the story leading up to the problem or struggle
- ☐ Choose one character from whom you learned a lesson.
- ☐ Write a struggle the character faced and what it taught you.

_____

_____

_____

_____

_____

_____

_____

_____

_____

_____

_____

_____

☐ Group Session   ☐ Class Session   ☐ Independent Reading

Readers Learn Lessons Alongside the Character

Choose your three most favorite books.
Think of the lesson the character learned and how it made an impact on you.

	Title	Struggle	Lesson
BOOK 1	_____	_____ _____ _____	_____ _____ _____
BOOK 2	_____	_____ _____ _____	_____ _____ _____
BOOK 3	_____	_____ _____ _____	_____ _____ _____

☐ Group Session   ☐ Class Session   ☐ Independent Reading

Readers Learn Lessons Alongside the Character

On your own:

Each paragraph should include:

☐ The title, author, and character's name.

☐ A brief background of the story leading up to the problem or struggle

☐ Choose one character from whom you learned a lesson.

☐ Write a struggle the character faced and what it taught you.

_____

_____

_____

_____

_____

_____

_____

_____

_____

_____

_____

Readers Dig into the Character's Conflict to Get a Better Understanding

☞ Answer in point form.

	External Conflict: 👧 Character vs. 👦 Character	
Name of Character	_____	_____
Conflict		
Proof #1 Action in Conflict		
Proof #2 Dialogue in Conflict		
Proof #3 Feelings in Conflict		
Trait Shown		

☐ Group Session   ☐ Class Session   ☐ Independent Reading

Readers Dig into the Character's Conflict to Get a Better Understanding

On your own:

Use the table on Page 85 to write a response.

Question: Write one external conflict the character experienced and what trait it showed.

Each paragraph should include:

- ☐ The title, author, and character's name.
- ☐ A brief background of the story leading up to the problem or struggle
- ☐ Choose an external conflict the character experienced
  - ⊛ Extra Credit: Proof of Conflict
- ☐ A theory \ trait shown

_____

_____

_____

_____

_____

_____

_____

_____

Readers Dig into the Character's Conflict to Get a Better Understanding

☞ Answer in point form.

External Conflict: Character vs. Character		
Name of Character	_____	_____
Conflict		
Proof #1 Action in Conflict		
Proof #2 Dialogue in Conflict		
Proof #3 Feelings in Conflict		
Trait Shown		

Readers Dig into the Character's Conflict to Get a Better Understanding

On your own:

Use the table on Page 87 to write a response.

Question: Write one external conflict the character experienced and what trait it showed.

Each paragraph should include:

☐ The title, author, and character's name.

☐ A brief background of the story leading up to the problem or struggle

☐ Choose an external conflict the character experienced.

　⭐ Extra Credit: Proof of Conflict

☐ A theory \ trait shown

_____

_____

_____

_____

_____

_____

_____

_____

Title: _____

Author: _____

Genre: _____

Teacher: _____

Readers Dig into the Character's Conflict to Get a Better Understanding

☞ Answer in point form.

	External Conflict: 👧 Character vs. 👩 Character	
Name of Character	_____	_____
Conflict		
Proof #1 Action in Conflict		
Proof #2 Dialogue in Conflict		
Proof #3 Feelings in Conflict		
Trait Shown		

☐ Group Session   ☐ Class Session   ☐ Independent Reading

Readers Dig into the Character's Conflict to Get a Better Understanding

On your own:

Use the table on Page 89 to write a response.

Question: Write one external conflict the character experienced and what trait it showed.

Each paragraph should include:

☐ The title, author, and character's name.

☐ A brief background of the story leading up to the problem or struggle

☐ Choose an external conflict the character experienced

    ★ Extra Credit: Proof of Conflict

☐ A theory \ trait shown

_____

_____

_____

_____

_____

_____

_____

_____

Readers Dig into the Character's Conflict to Get a Better Understanding

Internal Conflict: Character vs. Self		
Name of Character:		
	✋ One hand	✋ On the other hand
Conflict #1	_____ _____ _____	_____ _____ _____
Conflict #2	_____ _____ _____	_____ _____ _____
Resolution	_____ _____ _____	_____ _____ _____
Trait/Theory	_____	_____

Readers Dig into the Character's Conflict to Get a Better Understanding

📖 **On your own:**

Use the table on Page 91 to write a response.

Question: Write one internal conflict the character experienced and what trait it showed.

Each paragraph should include:

☐ The title, author, and character's name.

☐ A brief background of the story leading up to the problem or struggle

☐ Choose an internal conflict the character experienced.

    ⭐ Extra Credit: Resolutiont to the conflict

☐ A theory \ trait shown

_____

_____

_____

_____

_____

_____

_____

_____

_____

☐ Group Session   ☐ Class Session   ☐ Independent Reading

Readers Dig into the Character's Conflict to Get a Better Understanding

Internal Conflict: Character vs. Self		
Name of Character:		
	🖐 One hand	🖐 On the other hand
Conflict #1	_____ _____ _____	_____ _____ _____
Conflict #2	_____ _____ _____	_____ _____ _____
Resolution	_____ _____ _____	_____ _____ _____
Trait/Theory	_____	_____

☐ Group Session   ☐ Class Session   ☐ Independent Reading

Readers Dig into the Character's Conflict to Get a Better Understanding

On your own:

Use the table on Page 93 to write a response.

Question: Write one internal conflict the character experienced and what trait it showed.

Each paragraph should include:

☐ The title, author, and character's name.

☐ A brief background of the story leading up to the problem or struggle

☐ Choose an internal conflict the character experienced.

⊛ Extra Credit: Resolutiont to the conflict

☐ A theory \ trait shown

_____

_____

_____

_____

_____

_____

_____

_____

_____

Title: _____

Author: _____

Genre: _____

Teacher: _____

Readers Dig into the Character's Conflict to Get a Better Understanding

Internal Conflict: Character vs. Self		
Name of Character:		
	One hand	On the other hand
Conflict #1	_____ _____ _____	_____ _____ _____
Conflict #2	_____ _____ _____	_____ _____ _____
Resolution	_____ _____ _____	_____ _____ _____
Trait/Theory	_____	_____

Readers Dig into the Character's Conflict to Get a Better Understanding

On your own:

Use the table on Page 95 to write a response.

Question: Write one internal conflict the character experienced and what trait it showed.

Each paragraph should include:

☐ The title, author, and character's name.

☐ A brief background of the story leading up to the problem or struggle

☐ Choose an internal conflict the character experienced.

⊛ Extra Credit: Resolutiont to the conflict

☐ A theory \ trait shown

_____

_____

_____

_____

_____

_____

_____

_____

_____

Reading Response

✓ Checkbox: Writing should include

☐ The title, author, and character's name.   ☐ Restate and answer the question.

☐ A brief background of the story.   ☐ Two details that support your answer.

_____

_____

_____

_____

_____

_____

_____

_____

_____

_____

_____

_____

_____

_____

_____

☐ Group Session   ☐ Class Session   ☐ Independent Reading

Title: _____

Author: _____

Reading Response

☑ Checkbox: Writing should include

☐ The title, author, and character's name.

☐ A brief background of the story.

☐ Restate and answer the question.

☐ Two details <u>that support</u> your answer.

☐ Group Session   ☐ Class Session   ☐ Independent Reading

Reading Response

☑ Checkbox: Writing should include

☐ The title, author, and character's name.

☐ A brief background of the story.

☐ Restate and answer the question.

☐ Two details _that support_ your answer.

_____

_____

_____

_____

_____

_____

_____

_____

_____

_____

_____

_____

_____

_____

☐ Group Session   ☐ Class Session   ☐ Independent Reading